FRANCIS FRITH'S

KINGSTON UPON THAMES

PHOTOGRAPHIC MEMORIES

Patrick Loobey, born in 1947, has lived in Balham, Putney Southfields, Wandsworth and Streatham - all within the Borough of Wandsworth. He joined the Wandsworth Historical Society (founded in 1953) in 1969 and has served on its archaeological, publishing and management committees, serving as chairman from 1991 to 1994 and 1998 to 2001. Having collected Edwardian postcards and photographs of Wandsworth Borough and the surrounding areas for almost thirty years, he has a wide-ranging collection encompassing many local roads and subjects. This book complements other recent books by Patrick covering the Borough of Wandsworth and surrounding areas, notably 'Around Streatham' (1993, 1996, 2000, 2001); 'Battersea and Clapham' (1994 and 2000); 'Balham and Tooting' (1994 and 2001); 'Wandsworth' (1993, 1996, 1998); 'Wandsworth and Battersea at War' (1996 reprint 2001); 'Putney and Roehampton' (1988 and 1996); and 'Putney' (2001). Many more titles are forthcoming, including books on the theatres and cinemas of Wandsworth and Battersea, and transport in the Borough of Wandsworth.

FRANCIS FRITH'S
PHOTOGRAPHIC MEMORIES

KINGSTON UPON THAMES

PHOTOGRAPHIC MEMORIES

PATRICK LOOBEY

First published in the United Kingdom in 2004 by
Frith Book Company Ltd

Limited Hardback Subscribers Edition Published in 2004
ISBN 1-85937-910-9

Paperback Edition 2004
ISBN 1-85937-911-7

British Library Cataloguing in Publication Data

Francis Frith's Kingston upon Thames - Photographic Memories
Patrick Loobey

Frith Book Company Ltd
Frith's Barn, Teffont,
Salisbury, Wiltshire SP3 5QP
Tel: +44 (0) 1722 716 376
Email: info@francisfrith.co.uk
www.francisfrith.co.uk

Printed and bound in Great Britain

Front Cover: **KINGSTON UPON THAMES** *1906* 54709t
Frontispiece: **KINGSTON**, *High Street 1906* 54710

*The colour-tinting is for illustrative purposes only, and is not intended
to be historically accurate*

CONTENTS

FRANCIS FRITH
VICTORIAN PIONEER

FRANCIS FRITH, founder of the world-famous photographic archive, was a complex and multi-talented man. A devout Quaker and a highly successful Victorian businessman, he was philosophical by nature and pioneering in outlook.

By 1855 he had already established a wholesale grocery business in Liverpool, and sold it for the astonishing sum of £200,000, which is the equivalent today of over £15,000,000. Now a very rich man, he was able to indulge his passion for travel. As a child he had pored over travel books written by early explorers, and his fancy and imagination had been stirred by family holidays to the sublime mountain regions of Wales and Scotland. 'What lands of spirit-stirring and enriching scenes and places!' he had written. He was to return to these scenes of grandeur in later years to 'recapture the thousands of vivid and tender memories', but with a different purpose. Now in his thirties, and captivated by the new science of photography, Frith set out on a series of pioneering journeys up the Nile and to the Near East that occupied him from 1856 until 1860.

INTRIGUE AND EXPLORATION

These far-flung journeys were packed with intrigue and adventure. In his life story, written when he was sixty-three, Frith tells of being held captive by bandits, and of fighting 'an awful midnight battle to the very point of surrender with a deadly pack of hungry, wild dogs'. Wearing flowing Arab costume, Frith arrived at Akaba by camel sixty years before Lawrence of Arabia, where he encountered 'desert princes and rival sheikhs, blazing with jewel-hilted swords'.

He was the first photographer to venture beyond the sixth cataract of the Nile. Africa was still the mysterious 'Dark Continent', and Stanley and Livingstone's historic meeting was a decade into the future. The conditions for picture taking confound belief. He laboured for hours in his wicker dark-room in the sweltering heat of the desert, while the volatile chemicals fizzed dangerously in their trays. Back in London he exhibited his photographs and was 'rapturously cheered' by members of the Royal Society. His reputation as a photographer was made overnight.

VENTURE OF A LIFE-TIME

Characteristically, Frith quickly spotted the opportunity to create a new business as a specialist publisher of photographs. He lived in an era of immense and sometimes violent change. For the poor in the early part of Victoria's

reign work was exhausting and the hours long, and people had precious little free time to enjoy themselves. Most had no transport other than a cart or gig at their disposal, and rarely travelled far beyond the boundaries of their own town or village. However, by the 1870s the railways had threaded their way across the country, and Bank Holidays and half-day Saturdays had been made obligatory by Act of Parliament. All of a sudden the working man and his family were able to enjoy days out and see a little more of the world.

With typical business acumen, Francis Frith foresaw that these new tourists would enjoy having souvenirs to commemorate their days out. In 1860 he married Mary Ann Rosling and set out on a new career: his aim was to photograph every city, town and village in Britain. For the next thirty years he travelled the country by train and by pony and trap, producing fine photographs of seaside resorts and beauty spots that were keenly bought by millions of Victorians. These prints were painstakingly pasted into family albums and pored over during the dark nights of winter, rekindling precious memories of summer excursions.

THE RISE OF FRITH & CO

Frith's studio was soon supplying retail shops all over the country. To meet the demand he gathered about him a small team of photographers, and published the work of independent artist-photographers of the calibre of Roger Fenton and Francis Bedford. In order to gain some understanding of the scale of Frith's business one only has to look at the catalogue issued by Frith & Co in 1886: it runs to some 670 pages, listing not only many thousands of views of the British Isles but also many photographs of most European countries, and China, Japan, the USA and Canada - note the sample page shown on page 9 from the hand-written Frith & Co ledgers recording the pictures. By 1890 Frith had created the greatest specialist photographic publishing company in the world, with over 2,000 sales outlets - more than the combined number that Boots and WH Smith have today! The picture on the next page shows the Frith & Co display board at Ingleton in the Yorkshire Dales (left of window). Beautifully constructed with a mahogany frame and gilt inserts, it could display up to a dozen local scenes.

POSTCARD BONANZA

The ever-popular holiday postcard we know today took many years to develop. In 1870 the Post Office issued the first plain cards, with a pre-printed stamp on one face. In 1894 they allowed other publishers' cards to be sent through the mail with an attached adhesive halfpenny stamp. Demand grew rapidly, and in 1895 a new size of postcard was permitted called the court card, but there was little room for illustration. In 1899, a year after Frith's death, a new card measuring 5.5 x 3.5 inches became the standard format, but it was not until 1902 that the divided back came into being, so that the address and message could be on one face and a full-size illustration on the other. Frith & Co were in the vanguard of postcard development: Frith's sons Eustace and Cyril continued their father's monumental task, expanding the number of views offered to the public and recording more and more places in Britain, as the coasts and countryside were opened up to mass travel.

5					
6		St. Catherine's College	+		
7		Senate House & Library	+		
8				+	
9		Gerrard Hostel Bridge	+	+	+ +
3 0		Geological Museum			
1		Addenbrooke's Hospital	+		
2		St. Mary's Church	+		
3		Fitzwilliam Museum, Pitt Press &c	+		
4			+		
5	Buxton, The Crescent			+	
6		The Colonnade		+	
7		Public Gardens		+	
8				+	
9				+	
4 0	Haddon Hall, View from the Terrace			+	
	Miller's Dale			+	

Francis Frith had died in 1898 at his villa in Cannes, his great project still growing. The archive he created continued in business for another seventy years. By 1970 it contained over a third of a million pictures showing 7,000 British towns and villages.

FRANCIS FRITH'S LEGACY

Frith's legacy to us today is of immense significance and value, for the magnificent archive of evocative photographs he created provides a unique record of change in the cities, towns and villages throughout Britain over a century and more. Frith and his fellow studio photographers revisited locations many times down the years to update their views, compiling for us an enthralling and colourful pageant of British life and character.

We are fortunate that Frith was dedicated to recording the minutiae of everyday life. For it is this sheer wealth of visual data, the painstaking chronicle of changes in dress, transport, street layouts, buildings, housing, engineering and landscape that captivates us so much today. His remarkable images offer us a powerful link with the past and with the lives of our ancestors.

THE VALUE OF THE ARCHIVE TODAY

Computers have now made it possible for Frith's many thousands of images to be accessed almost instantly. Frith's images are increasingly used as visual resources, by social historians, by researchers into genealogy and ancestry, by architects and town planners, and by teachers involved in local history projects.

In addition, the archive offers every one of us an opportunity to examine the places where we and our families have lived and worked down the years. Highly successful in Frith's own era, the archive is now, a century and more on, entering a new phase of popularity. Historians consider the Francis Frith Collection to be of prime national importance. It is the only archive of its kind remaining in private ownership. Francis Frith's archive is now housed in an historic timber barn in the beautiful village of Teffont in Wiltshire. Its founder would not recognize the archive office as it is today. In place of the many thousands of dusty boxes containing glass plate negatives and an all-pervading odour of photographic chemicals, there are now ranks of computer screens. He would be amazed to watch his images travelling round the world at unimaginable speeds through internet lines.

The archive's future is both bright and exciting. Francis Frith, with his unshakeable belief in making photographs available to the greatest number of people, would undoubtedly approve of what is being done today with his lifetime's work. His photographs depicting our shared past are now bringing pleasure and enlightenment to millions around the world a century and more after his death.

KINGSTON UPON THAMES
AN INTRODUCTION

THE River Thames has been the highway of the hinterland of Surrey and Middlesex for thousands of years: the Romans used it for carrying their corn to London for export to Europe, and the Vikings for their raids into Saxon lands in the 8th and 9th centuries. The road system was not maintained for constant use, and long journeys by road were almost non-existent until the 19th century. By that time, the railways had earned a reputation for carrying the large quantities of materials and produce required for the expanding cities and towns.

Kingston market has been an important trading and meeting place for centuries. The earliest written record of it is in 1242, but the market probably dates from long before that, for it was laid out in 1170. The market town, where seven Saxon Kings are said to have been crowned, was granted its first charter in 1208; it soon became the centre for the exchanging of commodities and produce. The bridge at Kingston, first mentioned in 1193, was an important economic benefit to the area as goods of many types bound for London were transported through the town; the River Bridge was the only bridge upstream of London Bridge until 1729.

What is now referred to as South-West London was until recently the arable countryside of Surrey, supplying fruit and vegetables to the ever-increasing population of London. As the inner London Boroughs grew, the hinterland of Surrey was to remain an agriculturally based economy for many years. These Thames-side parishes had depended on the river for their commerce for thousands of years, transporting stone, timber and agricultural products to their larger neighbour, London, downstream.

The royal accounts at Hampton Court relate the continuous use of the river for communication. Kings chose the riverside for their palaces at Richmond and Hampton Court and other royal residences at Kew. The large parks in south-west London were mainly laid out as royal deer parks: Nonsuch near Cheam was made for the pleasure of Henry VII in the late 15th century, and Richmond Park for Charles I in 1637. Hampton Court Park and Bushey Park were both associated with Hampton Court Palace.

Industry in the Kingston area was sparse, as agriculture was the mainstay of commerce right into the 20th century. Breweries were probably the largest employers on the riverfront at Mortlake, Richmond and Kingston. Industry was largely based on the riverfront at Kingston in the 19th century, as the wharves handled the commodities exported via the river to London. Tanning and candle factories lined the river alongside the Thames Bridge into the 1960s. Large-scale industry was only introduced to the area in the 20th century with firms like the Sopwith aeroplane factory, which became Hawkers in the 1920s; this immense factory on the riverside closed in the 1990s. The riverside was chosen in 1948 for the local authority power station, but this closed in 1980 and was finally demolished in 1994. A housing estate was built on the site.

With the advent of steam power, horses no longer had to use the towpaths to pull the barges along; and so the riverside gardens at Canbury were built and improved at the end of the 19th century. Flood and tidal controls on the Thames were introduced with the building of locks at Richmond, Teddington and Hampton.

After a series of cholera epidemics in London during the 1840s the Vauxhall and Lambeth Water Co were obliged to install filter beds and pumping stations at Hampton, taking their water from above Teddington lock rather than at Battersea. Much land at Hampton on both banks of the Thames was taken for the filter beds and reservoirs, thus denying public access to the river.

Besides industry the river was used from the mid-19th century for sporting activities and boat building at Teddington, Hampton,

Richmond and Kingston. Instead of barges, the river was thronged with new kinds of craft for yachting and sculling.

The scene and pace of life of all of this area was changed with the coming of the steam railway in the 1840s. The railway was the greatest impetus to the expansion of suburbia, as developers quickly seized on the opportunity to buy up agricultural land for housing; many of older great estates were broken up and parcelled out for building. As the railway companies expanded further into Surrey,

KINGSTON UPON THAMES, *The Thames c1955* K32032

11

the house developers were not slow in buying up agricultural and parkland near the proposed railway stations. Teddington, Hampton and Surbiton were small villages before the housing construction gangs arrived in the late 19th century.

With the improvement in transport facilities - trams came in 1906 and trolley buses in the 1930s – there was a resurgence in construction. The 1930s saw housing development at Tolworth, mainly after the opening of Kingston by-pass in 1927. New methods of entertainment were built for these expanded villages and new dormitory towns in the form of cinemas, theatres and dance halls. The competition with television has seen many of these venues close or transformed into new uses since the 1960s.

Kingston is now renowned as a shopping centre with the large Bentalls store at its heart.

The John Lewis development at the Bentall Centre shopping precinct took five years to construct, while a new road scheme was also built in the centre of the town. This included the pedestrianisation of the heart of the town: Clarence Street is now for pedestrians only, with traffic diverted underneath or around the new scheme. Thanks to the developers, there has been a great loss of historic buildings throughout the 20th century in the centre of Kingston, and many fine timber-framed buildings have been lost.

With the reorganisation and enlargement of Greater London in 1963, the former north east Surrey towns of Sutton, Kingston, Wimbledon, Merton and Mitcham have become London Boroughs, and Twickenham has been joined with Richmond to form another of these new boroughs.

Bentalls Corner c1960 K32058

THE TOWN CENTRE

KINGSTON UPON THAMES *1906* 54709

The Coronation Stone was recovered in 1730 from the collapsed chapel of St Mary that abutted All Saints' Church and then used as a mounting block for horsemen in the Market Square. The stone was 'rediscovered' in the early 19th century and placed outside the Municipal Offices. The decorative setting for the stone bears the names of seven Saxon Kings supposed to have been crowned at Kingston: Edward the Elder, Athelstan, Edmund, Eadred, Eadwig, Edward the Martyr and Etheldred the Unready. The only Kings for whom there is solid evidence that they were crowned at Kingston are Athelstan in AD924 and Etheldred in 978.

▼ *The Coronation Stone c1955* K32017

The Coronation Stone was placed upon a stone plinth set within decorative railings right in the heart of Kingston outside the Kingston municipal offices in 1850, but as traffic increased in the 20th century it was moved back from the roadway in 1935. The stone is now sited as we see it here, alongside the Clattern Bridge over the Hogsmill River outside the Guildhall.

▶ *Market Place c1950*
K32027

The small green was the site of the Coronation Stone [from 1850 until it was re-sited outside the Guildhall. We can see people taking the opportunity of resting from their Saturday morning shopping expedition while waiting for a bus. The Old Post House restaurant and tea shop (left), claiming a date of 1346 in this photograph, was actually of 16th century date; it had once been the Crane Inn, and was last known as the Old Curiosity Shop before its demolition in 1954.

High Street 1906 54710

The town of Kingston was awarded County Town status in 1893, which it retained even after becoming a London Borough in 1964. However, the County Town status has now gone to Woking, and any remaining County Council staff will be relocated across the county by 2007. Behind the Coronation Stone (centre) are the Municipal Offices, which were replaced by the Guildhall in 1935. As this is a market town, the town centre has a remarkable number of hotels and hostelries; on the right is the Griffin Hotel, established in the 16th century, an important posting house that closed in 1986 and was converted into shops. A proud early motorist stands outside the Assembly Rooms (right).

Market Day 1906
54706

There has probably been a formal market at Kingston since at least Saxon times; a series of charters have been granted by royalty since the 13th century, giving it official status. The charter granted by King Charles I gave Kingston the right to ban any other market within seven miles; this right has been used in recent times to stop markets operating in Putney, a little over four miles away. The Market Hall was opened in 1840.

The Market Place 1890
27208

A close inspection of the shops to either side of the Market Hall reveals their late medieval origins. The plots are small, and to use the land to its best advantage the owners have built upwards, not quite like a modern skyscraper but daring for its time. The small independent trader was able to increase his earnings by renting the upper floors – an example is the hairdresser's salon in the right-hand side background. Transport was still dependent on the horse, and the pedestrian had to be careful crossing the roadway so as to avoid the droppings.

▼ *The Market Place 1948* K32016

It is Saturday in Kingston Market Place, and swarms of shoppers have descended to see the fresh produce on offer that might supplement the wartime rationing that was still in force. Did many of these people consider that the Market Place was the scene for punishment of miscreants in the past? In 1572 'rogues and vagabonds' were whipped around the market place and their ears branded. The stocks and pillory were placed beside the Town Hall, which later became the Market Hall.

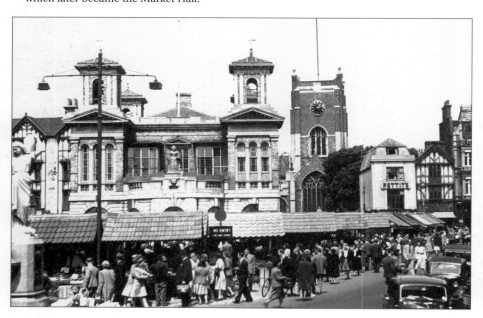

▶ *The Market Place c1960* K32096

Countrywide shops that one could see in almost any town gradually superseded the small family retail outlets. The plastic fascias of these shops have no individuality to them, and make towns look very similar. Here, Dorothy Perkins (centre right) and a Wimpey bar serving hamburgers (centre right) have arrived in the Market Place, where shoppers are eager to snap up the fresh produce on offer.

◄ *The Market Place, the Shrubsole Memorial c1955* K32048

The statue of a water carrier above the drinking fountain is rather apt. The fountain was erected in 1882 in memory of Henry Shrubsole, three times mayor of Kingston, who died suddenly while distributing tea to the aged poor in 1880. In 1866, Henry and John Shrubsole had bought a shop in the Market Place and reorganised it to department store status, thus bringing shoppers to Kingston who would previously have gone to London. The shop bore their name, then became Hide's department store from 1873 until 1977, when it was bought by House of Fraser.

► *The Market Place c1955* K32068

A lorry delivering Whitworth's Self Raising Flour negotiates the traffic and shoppers. The parking meter was yet to rear its ugly shape in Kingston, and car owners jostle for parking space. The Market Hall, built in 1840, was refurbished and repaired in 1995, re-opening as the Tourist Information Office and a cafeteria.

▶ *The Market Place c1955* K32046

The three-storey building of Boots the Chemist at Nos 15 and 16 Market Place is not as old as it seems. A quick look back at the 1890 view of the market place will show the building's original appearance; it was altered between 1909 and 1929 to give it that 'olde worlde charm' - the timber framing has only been applied to the surface of the walls. The plasterwork figures also date from the 20th century; they include the Kings and Queens associated with Kingston's history, and the town's coat of arms. The smaller building to the left dates from the 1570s.

◀ *All Saints' Parish Church 1906* 54715

The earliest reference to a church at Kingston tells of the crowning of Saxon kings and a Great Council taking place in the 9th century. There is some possible Saxon dressed stonework surviving in the fabric of the church. The Sheriff of Surrey, Gilbert the Norman, built a large church here between 1120 and 1130, but few scant remains survive of this cruciform structure; the Victorians managed to remove and destroy a Norman doorway. A new nave was built in 1370, and the church was enlarged in the 15th century. The Victorians enlarged the transepts and carried out alterations to the internal fabric of the tower.

▲ *The Parish Church, the Interior 1893* 31774

The Queen came here in her Jubilee year, 1977, to unveil a stone commemorating the crowning of her predecessor Edward the Elder on this site 1100 years ago. Egbert, King of Wessex, held his great council here in 838, and Athelstan and Ethelred the Unready were two of the Saxon kings of England crowned here in the 10th century. The church has a 14th-century wall painting of St Blaise, and the impressive 16th-century tomb of Sir Anthony Benn; the 17th-century marble font is attributed to Sir Christopher Wren. In the tower are twelve bells and an 18th-century carillon. The great west window is 19th-century, and the magnificent Frobenius organ was installed in 1988.

◄ *Bentalls Corner c1965*
K32058

Kingston is well renowned as a shopping centre of excellence, with Bentalls department store in Clarence Street at its hub. The store first opened in 1863 as a small draper's shop, and it expanded over the years. The six-storey store we see here, designed by Sir Aston Webb & Son, who had also designed Kingston Guildhall, was built in 1936. The intention was to emulate an Italian Renaissance palace and Hampton Court Palace.

▲ *Clarence Street c1965* K32108

Bentalls department store is in a commanding position, and towers over the other shops in Clarence Street. The Duchess of Clarence, later Queen Adelaide to King William IV, opened the present Kingston Bridge in 1828. Her name was given to this street, which was previously called London Road.

▶ **DETAIL FROM** K32108

The Water Splash 1906 K54725

The Hogsmill River runs through the heart of Kingston, and once supported five water mills. The water splash was just upstream from where the Guildhall now stands, and where St James' Road and Penrhyn Road joined. While horses and carts had to wade through the river, giving the animals the chance for a drink and expanding any loose joints in the wooden wheels during hot weather, pedestrians had the pleasure of a raised walkway past the ford. The ford was bridged in 1938 and hidden beneath the College roundabout in 1987.

THE RIVER THAMES

The Bridge 1951 K32002

A bridge was first built at Kingston in 1219; it was the first above London Bridge until Putney Bridge was opened in 1729. The present structure, designed by Edward Lappidge, was opened in 1828 and widened in 1914. In 2000 the original bridge was strengthened and a new bridge built alongside to widen the carriageway by 6.6 metres. The one item removed in the early 1960s was the trolley bus poles.

The Bridge 1896
38327A

A relatively uncluttered view of the parish church could be had from the bridge. The medieval bridge was slightly downstream from the present structure, and the stone footings and approach were uncovered in archaeological excavations in 1986 before the construction of the new John Lewis store.

The Bridge 1906 54717

The advent of the railways in the mid 19th century was to enhance the use of the Thames for pleasure as day-trippers took to the water in punts and sailing boats. Some men would take to the water first thing in the morning, rowing for a while before leaving for work in the City of London. From the mid 20th century the Thames was used less for industry, with fewer barges and tugs and fewer wharves for industry on its banks, giving ample room for sailing and pleasure boats.

▶ *The Bridge 1906* 54718

As the popularity of the Thames at Kingston increased, provision was made to cater for the increasing numbers. Tea-rooms, small restaurants, public landing places and hotels were built, as we can see from the notices on the Surrey shore: 'Bond's Sun Hotel', 'Luncheons, Teas, Dinners', and 'Public Landing'. The Sun Hotel's garden reached right down to the river.

◄ *The Yacht Basin 1906*
54719

The river upstream from Kingston Bridge was largely free from commercial traffic, and consequently safer for yachtsmen. The river also gains from the wide expanse of open ground at Hampton Court, where the wind (coming mainly from the south west) is unimpeded by buildings. The chimney (right) is part of Fricker's Eagle brewery with a wharf on the riverside.

The Wharf c1955
K32012

The few waterside industries of Kingston were based off the High Street with their wharves backing onto the Thames. Hide's department store has an advertising hoarding on the riverfront (left) proclaiming their fabrics and furnishings. The large roof beyond the Hides hoarding is that of the Odeon cinema in the High Street, which was demolished in 1988.

▶ *From the Bridge 1896* 38322

The Thames is crowded with all sorts of small craft; it is probably a bank holiday. Both shores are packed with people enjoying the sunshine. To the left is the Sun Hotel landing stage and gardens, and beyond is the gable-ended boatyard of Alfred Burgoine, founded in the 1860s and famous for their fast sailing yachts. The firm lasted until it went into receivership in 1910 and closed down.

◀ *The River 1950* K32011

Empty barges waiting to be towed back down the river are tied up at the embankment alongside the Portsmouth Road where it becomes the High Street.

▲ *Riverside Promenade 1951* K32010

Small private launches are moored alongside the promenade. A couple take a relaxing stroll along the riverside promenade away from the constant traffic noise nearby.

◄ *The Thames c1955*
K32038

A Girl Guide troop is enjoying the sunshine on the riverbank upstream of the bridge. As earnings grew after the Second World War and holiday entitlements increased, there was time to enjoy the simple pleasures of the non-tidal Thames.

◀ *The Tamesis Club 1890* 23551

The Tamesis has had a premier role in the development of dinghy racing on the River Thames. It was founded in 1885, with the first clubroom at Alfred Burgoine's boathouse here at Hampton Wick, where club members moored their boats. The coming of the railway in 1870 opened the river to commuters and pleasure boaters, increasing the use of gigs, dinghies and canoes. The Tamesis Club joined with four other river sailing clubs to form the Sailing Boat Association in 1888, and was responsible for formulating many of the rules. The river sailing season began each year with the Easter regatta at the Tamesis Club.

◀ *On the River c1950*
K32022

Most of the Thames
passenger pleasure
launches were steam
powered up to the
Second World War and
were converted to diesel
engines afterwards. The
1950s saw an increase in
day trips, as people who
might not have had the
money available for
holidays could afford the
odd day out on the
Thames. The 'Clifton
Castle', fully loaded, is
heading downstream.

◀ *The River c1955*
K32020

Hart & Co (centre left)
advertise their skiffs,
dinghies and canoes for
hire from their riverside
boathouses nearer
Surbiton. Only a light
breeze is blowing for the
small dinghies on the
Thames.

▲ *On the River 1896* 38342

The paddle steamer SS 'Queen Elizabeth' sails majestically past the houseboats along the Thames near Hampton Court. This large vessel sank at its moorings at Kew on 5 September 1904.

▶ **DETAIL FROM** 38342

The Thames c1955
K32032

Young anglers are hoping for a big catch. The chestnut paling in the background was used as a temporary replacement for the iron railings which were removed for scrap salvage during the Second World War; similar railings could be seen around most public parks and gardens up to the late 1950s.

Downstream from the Railway Bridge 1890 23552

Work on buildings up the foreshore (the Barge Walk) is in progress behind the hopeful anglers. On the Hampton Wick side, hidden by the trees, are Walnut Tree House and Grove Cottage, with Wick Lodge Boathouse just beyond the motor launches.

▶ *Canbury Gardens 1906*
54722

Canbury Gardens was laid out along the old towpath beside the Thames downstream of Kingston railway bridge in 1889-91, and opened to the public in 1890.

◀ *Canbury Gardens 1906* 54721

Two soldiers relax on a bench next to the bandstand in the sunlight at Canbury Gardens, downstream of Kingston railway bridge. The army barracks was based not far away, just off Kings Road. It opened in 1875, covering 16 acres of land; it was the central depot for the East Surrey Regiment, later renamed the Queen's Royal Surreys. The barracks closed in 1959. One wonders if the children are discussing the way to find Alice's little secret wonderland.

▲ *Canbury Gardens 1891* 29660

The bandstand at Canbury Gardens was a gift to the people of Kingston from a former mayor, C E Nuthall. The bandstand was removed in the 1950s, but a replacement has been installed. Free concerts are given nowadays on Sundays at the bandstand.

◄ *Canbury Gardens 1893* 31771

Recently planted trees and shrubs line the riverside pathway of the newly opened gardens. The gardens now have tennis courts, a bowling green and children's playgrounds.

▼ *The River at Surbiton 1896* 38325

Here we see a classic late Victorian scene: people are enjoying the relaxing waters of the Thames in a skiff. However, such pleasures were really only available to those middle-class people that could afford the time to spend in this fashion.

▶ **SURBITON**
Messenger's Boat House 1896 38336

A Thames sailing barge is being unloaded. The heavily-laden 'Glasgow' (the barge on the left) has to wait, while the ship alongside the landing place is unloaded via a horse and cart driven into the water. The towpath for barges and sailing ships was mainly on the Surrey bank of the river. These sailing barges were still in commercial operation well into the 1960s.

The Promenade 1906 54720

The Portsmouth Road runs alongside the river. A horse-drawn bus is packed with passengers - the top deck of a bus was the favoured choice for tourists in fine weather. The Edwardian era enjoyed a period of good summers that saw an increase in excursions and use of the river amenities. The promenade was built in the 1850s with material excavated from the reservoir in Portsmouth Road by the Chelsea Water Works.

▶ SURBITON
St Raphael's Church, Portsmouth Road 1893 31770

Alexander Raphael, a devout Roman Catholic, was an important landowner who lived at Surbiton Place. He was the first Catholic Lord Mayor of London since the reformation, and St Raphael's was the first Catholic Church to be built in Kingston since this time. The Bishop of Southwark consecrated the chapel, which was designed by Charles Parker, in 1848. The estate was sold off after Alexander's death, and by 1855 a number of cottages and houses had been built in what are now Westfield Road, St Leonard's Road, and Cadogan Road.

SURBITON

SURBITON, *The Cutting c1950* S231008

This wide cutting for the railway was constructed in the 1830s by hundreds of navvies, who removed the side of Surbiton Hill and deposited the spoil at Ditton embankment. The heart-stirring site of steam engines hauling through Surbiton Station became just a memory when steam traction was removed from the southern section of British Railways in 1967.

▼ **SURBITON,** *King Charles Road 1907* 58266

Surbiton Common was the scene of one of the last episodes of the English Civil War in 1648. The war was but all over when a Surrey-led rebellion of Royalists, with many recruited from Kingston, were attacked by Parliamentary forces on the common. Lord Francis Villiers, younger brother of the Duke of Buckingham, was killed in the skirmish. Villiers Road and King Charles Road were named after this battle.

► **SURBITON**
Victoria Road
c1950 S231019

A learner driver is making his way warily through Victoria Road, with the largest vehicle he would encounter probably being a Kingston-bound trolley bus (just visible in the distance). Timothy Whites the chemist (left) was a nation-wide outlet competing with the far larger Boots, who were to subsume them in the 1960s.

◄ **SURBITON**
Brighton Road
c1950 S231021

The late Victorian era saw the development of shopping parades. The one on the left was built in 1904-05, when electricity came to Surbiton, so it was given the name Electric Parade. Parking restrictions were yet to descend upon Surbiton, and the few drivers after the Second World War have the roads to themselves. Many local authorities were to save ratepayers the expense of erecting lamp posts by attaching their street lamps to the trolley poles, as we see here. Philpott and Co at No 40 on the right supplied stationery.

► **SURBITON**
Claremont Road
c1955 S231028

The rather grand clock tower (centre left) was built to commemorate the coronation of Edward VII in 1902, but it was not unveiled until 1908, and an inscription was never added. The trolley buses were introduced in 1937 and withdrawn from service in 1961; the trolley poles were removed shortly after. There is a strange contrast of building styles here, with

late Victorian on the right and late 1930s opposite. When the Coutts family took over the development of the Kingston New Town in 1844, they set about renaming many of the streets; Claremont Road had been Railway Road up to this time.

SURBITON
Hook Road c1955
S231041

Two RAC patrolmen saunter past the Hook Road post office (right), ignoring the few motor vehicles on the road. Petrol was still expensive after the war, and was soon to be rationed again during the Suez crisis of 1956.

HAMPTON WICK AND HAMPTON COURT

HAMPTON WICK, *High Street c1960* H401003

Old Bridge Street on the right once led to Kingston Bridge, which was a little bit downstream of the modern bridge. The cat's-cradle of wires was for the electricity pick up on the trolley buses en route to Twickenham from Kingston. The small antiques shops similar to the one on the left, Discoveries, have largely disappeared today.

► **HAMPTON WICK**
High Street c1960
H401001

The High Street appears quiet with very little traffic; a road sweeper on the left goes about filling his three-wheeled rubbish cart. The few small shops on the right include the Magolia Restaurant , a car hire shop and E Lawrence, a tobacconist's. The London Co-op store in the background is having some rubbish removed via the drop-sided van outside.

◄ **HAMPTON WICK**
The River below Kingston 1890
23541

Private boathouses line the river, and well manicured lawns sweep down to the water.

▲ **HAMPTON COURT,** *The Palace 1899* 43045

This is the south-east front, designed by Sir Christopher Wren and built between 1689 and 1700. The palace was built by Cardinal Wolsey in the early 16th century, but seeing his sovereign's displeasure, Wolsey was forced to offer the magnificent palace to Henry VIII. Five of Henry's wives lived here at some point; Anne Boleyn spent her honeymoon at Hampton Court during its construction. William III and his Queen, Mary, instructed Christopher Wren to rebuild and remodel the Tudor palace and landscape its surroundings. The overwhelming grandeur of Hampton Court's thousand rooms, its royal art collection, its formal gardens and its yew maze leave an unforgettable impression on visitors.

◄ **HAMPTON COURT** *The Palace c1955* H17055

The Great Gate House, dating from Cardinal Wolsey's time, originally had two more storeys, but they were removed in 1771-73. The facing bricks date mainly from an 1880s restoration. The Moat Bridge was installed by Henry VIII to replace an earlier one.

HAMPTON COURT, *The Palace c1955* H17057

The stone drawbridge entrance to the Great Gatehouse to the palace was buried when Charles II had the moat filled in. The Ministry of Works had the moat dug out again in 1909-10, and discovered Henry VIII's bridge. It lacked the parapets on either side, which were rebuilt, together with the supporters of the royal arms, known as the King's Beasts. The Beasts were renewed in 1950.

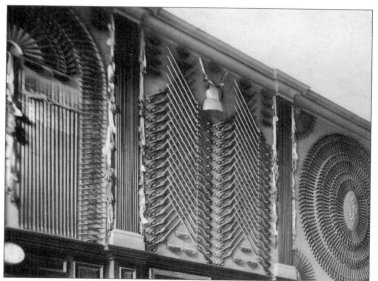

▲ **HAMPTON COURT**
*The Palace, The Guard Chamber
1890* 27272

The King's Guard Chamber contains one of
the world's greatest displays of weaponry.
Entrance to the private and state
apartments was not granted by the
Yeoman of the Guard until the visitor had
passed through the King's Guard Chamber.
Here undoubtedly ambassadors,
emissaries and other distinguished visitors
were challenged and searched for
weapons. With the display of over 3000
arms laid out in a decorative pattern by
William III's gunsmith Harris, anyone
attempting mischief would have been put

◄ **DETAIL FROM** 27272

► HAMPTON COURT
The Palace, The Lion Gates c1960 H17067

Those who come to Hampton Court Palace by way of Bushy Park or from Kingston enter through the Lion Gates, which face the end of the splendid avenue of chestnut trees. This approach gains its name from the carved lions on the piers. Queen Anne built the gates, and carved on the columns are her initials. The wrought-iron work is very fine, and is believed to have been done by the French master of wrought iron work, Tijou. In the upper panels the letter' G', which stands for King George, has replaced the 'A'. The famous maze is just inside the Lion Gates.

◄ HAMPTON COURT
The Gardens c1960 H17115

There are over 60 acres of gardens at the palace; these were begun by Cardinal Wolsey in the 16th century and remodelled by William III and Mary II in the Baroque manner. The great vine and the maze are the two most popular items to visit, but there is also the orangery, the Tudor garden, and the privy garden, restored in 1995. To the south of the palace are the Pond Gardens. These three sunken gardens were originally ornamental ponds used for holding freshwater fish until they were needed in the kitchens for cooking. Today they have been transformed with impressive displays of spring and summer bedding.

◀ **HAMPTON COURT**
The Long Water 1890
27274

Beyond the east front gardens is Home Park with the great canal, or Long Water, dug for Charles II in the 1660s. The lake is one mile in length, and tench and carp have been caught here. The park contains a herd of 270 deer, a golf course founded in the 19th century, and an oak tree from the original park, which is probably over 1,000 years old.

HAMPTON COURT
On the River 1896
38341

The passenger launch SS 'Queen Elizabeth' has almost beached to disembark and take on board passengers. A gangplank has been laid to the foreshore. In the background is the third bridge at Hampton, opened in 1865; its wrought iron lattice girders of five spans were replaced with the present bridge in 1933.

◄ HAMPTON COURT
The Tea Gardens c1965
H17077

A full day is not enough to understand all of the history and building styles of Hampton Court Palace, and many families take a breather at the tea gardens cafeteria.

◄ **HAMPTON COURT**
The Deer in Bushey Park c1960 K32053

Cardinal Wolsey had the 1,100 acres enclosed in 1514. When Henry VIII acquired the Wolsey estates, he quickly stocked Bushey Park with deer as part of his vast hunting grounds, and had a wall built by 1540 to ensure that the game was kept for him. Charles II instigated a tree-planting programme and the building of the Long Water. Lord Halifax rebuilt Bushey House in the early 18th century. Bushey Park was the base for General Eisenhower when planning the D-Day operation in 1944, and Home Park welcomes thousands of visitors during the annual Hampton Court Flower Show in July.

◄ **HAMPTON**
St Mary's Church 1890 23556

The church of St Mary at Hampton was rebuilt in 1831 to the designs of Edward Lappidge. The old medieval church was too small to cope with the increasing number of worshippers. The church is built in plain yellow/white stock brick with small lancet windows.
The west tower is also of brick. Sir Arthur Blomfield added a sanctuary to the east end in 1888. To the right is Garrick's Ait, or island.

HAMPTON
The High Street c1950
H369002

The village of Hampton is quite compact and largely ignored by those rushing through in their cars. Beyond the car on the right is the sign for the Jolly Coopers public house, now the oldest in Hampton, still on its original site and within its original building. The Jolly Gardeners pub (near right) was closed in 1955, and has been used since by the Heath family, the boat builders. Barclays Bank on the left was built in 1908.

▲ **HAMPTON,** *Thames Street c1950* H369004

The parish church of St Mary is still the tallest building in Hampton. As car ownership increased in the 1960s and 1970s, the shops in Hampton were gradually closed; the premises were found to be more valuable to be converted as housing than for selling groceries, fruit or vegetables.

HAMPTON
The River c1955
H369008

A sailing regatta is admired from the riverside benches. The four-wheeled perambulator was considered the Rolls Royce of prams for young children in the immediate post-war period, but they are a very rare site in the 21st century. On the far side of the river is Hurst Park racecourse and grandstand.

EAST MOLESEY, *Hampton Court Way c1955* H17068

Hampton Court Railway Station (left) was built in 1849 by the London & South Western Railway Co to accommodate the increasing number of visitors to Hampton Court after it opened to the public in 1838. The shopping parade was built after the new Thames bridge at Hampton Court was opened in 1933.

▲ **HAMPTON COURT,** *Molesey Weir c1965* H17073

The weir at Molesey was constructed to control the level of water higher up the river. The walkway across the weir can be considered a little bit of fun, but it is not for the faint-hearted.

◄ **EAST MOLESEY**
Coming over the Rollers 1896 38346

On the left are the four rollers which allow
smaller craft to negotiate the weir. The
passengers had to disembark and push
and pull the punt or canoe over the rollers
instead of going through the lock - that
was more for larger craft, such as the small
steam pinnace on the right.

◄ **DETAIL FROM** 38346

EAST MOLESEY
Steamboats in the Lock 1896 38350

The lock is filled to capacity with small steamboats and punts waiting for the waters to subside and then pass on their way. The larger craft on the left is well furnished with food hampers and two young maids to help serve at table. On top of the boat are some well dressed ladies and gentlemen. The locks, just upstream of Hampton Court, were first built in 1815.

AROUND AND ABOUT KINGSTON

TOLWORTH, *Tolworth Tower c1965* T263056

The A3 Kingston by-pass, the first modern by-pass in Britain, was built in 1927 to alleviate the constant traffic flow through the town on the Portsmouth Road. An underpass now speeds the traffic along the A3 through the intersection. The tower block was built in 1963; it is 75 metres tall and has a radio station transmitter antenna on top. Plans for a 120-bed Travelodge hotel in Tolworth Tower have been given the go-ahead recently by councillors. The hotel and cafe bar should be built by May 2005 in the Ewell Road tower's seven-storey north wing. The lower area is a Marks and Spencer store.

TOLWORTH
The Toby Jug c1965 T263032

The Toby Jug public house was built soon after the A3 Kingston by-pass was opened in 1927. The pub was sited alongside the roadway to gain trade from the increasing amount of traffic heading for Portsmouth and the south coast. The pub was demolished about 2003 for a mixed retail and residential development of the 3.5 ha (8.9 acres) site adjacent to the Kingston by-pass. The site, comprising the Charrington Bowl and the Toby Jug, was owned by Six Continents Retail; it was sold to Tesco for a superstore to be opened within the following 2 to 3 years. Bass have insisted that its proposed Toby Jug development will not increase traffic.

TOLWORTH, *The Broadway c1965* T263029

The Broadway shopping parade was built in the 1930s with easy access for pedestrians. However, thanks to its position as a main route to the A3, traffic has increased; the thoroughfare has been cut in two by a central barrier, so that pedestrians now have to use an underpass. In the distance is the Odeon cinema, opened in 1934 and closed by 1959. It was demolished, and Tolworth Tower was built on the site in 1963.

TOLWORTH
The Broadway c1955
T262028

With the opening of the Kingston by-pass in 1927, housing development gathered pace; by 1931, 6.5 miles of roads had carved across the farmland and arable fields for the erection of 1,300 houses and 57 shops to accommodate 1,300 residents, with over 600 more houses planned for that year. What had been a small hamlet had within four years become a small dormitory town of its own.

► **NEW MALDEN**
Malden Road
c1955 N167067

The police station (right) on the corner of Malden Road and Burlington Road was opened in 1892. The roadway just had a few large private houses, until developers inserted the shopping parades and widened the carriageway in the 1930s. The undertaker Frederick W Paine (right) has an apt name for that necessary trade.

◄ **NEW MALDEN**
High Street c1965
N167062

A contrast of building styles greets the eye as Late Victorian Queen Anne meets neo-Georgian from the 1920s, and early 1950s severity jostles with 1930s mock-Tudor on the left. New Malden had a spurt of building expansion after the railway arrived here in 1847.

▲ **MALDEN,** *The Plough Inn c1955* O140338

The 15th-century Plough Inn is considered to be the second centre of Old Malden; the immediate area around the parish church, behind the photographer in Church Road, was the centre of the Saxon village. The Plough Green alongside the inn has a yearly village fete.

◄ **OLD MALDEN**
The Pond c1955
O140365

The old Plough Inn is to the right of the pond where two little girls are feeding the ducks. The mock Tudor suburban shops in Malden Road were an addition built in the 1930s. Notice the sunblinds at Rendells the butcher's and a few neighbouring shops. The sign placed in the pond warns that 'Persons throwing rubbish in pond will be prosecuted', but neglects to inform us who will do the prosecuting!

MORDEN
Abbotsbury Road
c1953 M359019

The variety of shops in Morden was to alter after the underground railway station opened in 1926 and large-scale retail development began. Shoppers before this time had to make their way to Wimbledon, Croydon or Kingston. The housewife in the 1950s had a daily trip to the shops, as the private ownership of refrigerators was fairly low, and dairy products and meat could not be kept for long. Saturday was the busiest shopping day, as weekly wages were still paid in cash on Fridays, enabling the household necessities to be bought; there was always the chance of an end-of-week display bargain to be had.

MORDEN
*Looking North-East
c1965* M359055

Crown House provides a view of London Road and Morden Court and the slightly earlier mock Tudor York Close to the left. In preparation behind Morden Court is a car parking area, and beyond that are the carriage sheds for the Northern Line underground. A few of the remaining Victorian houses in Morden can be glimpsed at the bottom right.

▲ **TEDDINGTON,** *The Anglers Hotel*
1891 23538

Teddington was earlier called Todynton
and Tuddington. It is the site of the first
lock on the Thames, which has been
rebuilt in masonry, with a subsidiary lock
for the passage of pleasure boats. The
river is at this point scarcely affected by
the tides, which are two hours later than
at London Bridge, and the low and high
water levels are respectively 16½ and 1½
feet higher, the bed of the river rising
about one foot per mile. Robert Porter
opened his boatyard here in 1891 (right);
it became Porter & Brice by 1895, but did
not survive beyond 1910. The Anglers Inn
with its slipway and landing stairs is to
the left of the Albion boathouse. The ferry,
although largely superseded by
construction of the footbridge in 1889,
was operated here until about 1950.

► **DETAIL FROM** 23538

▲ TEDDINGTON
The Bridge 1899 43051

An obelisk 265 yards below the lock marks the boundary of the jurisdiction of the Port of London Authority and the Environment Agency. Before Teddington Lock was constructed in 1811, the river was tidal as far as Kingston. The pound lock was an early attempt to control the high tides, which in the 19th century were around ten feet above the level in Roman times. Today the tide flows up to Teddington, but the half tide lock at Richmond prevents too strong a current and keeps the river level. In 1888-89 this footbridge was built to the designs of G Pooley, and replaced the ferry at Teddington. Two footbridges of different designs meet on the island here.
The bridge spanning the river from the Middlesex bank to the island is a suspension bridge, while the shorter structure crossing from the Surrey bank has a girder design.

◀ **DETAIL FROM** 43051

77

TEDDINGTON
The Parish Church
1899 43055

The north aisle of the St Mary's Church, in red brick with diaper work, dates from the early Tudor period. The rest, including the brick tower, dates mainly from 1753-54, except for the 19th-century chancel. The church was found to be too small for the increasing population; with the opening of St Alban's in 1889 as the new parish church, St Mary's was relegated to secondary use, but in 1967 it was again made the parish church.

TEDDINGTON, *St Alban's Church 1899* 43056

The vicar of St Mary's, F Leith Lloyd, wanted a larger church for his congregation, and engaged William Niven to design this enormous church at a cost of £30,000. It looks like a Gothic cathedral with its flying buttresses; an intended west tower was never built. The church was consecrated in 1896 and unveiled as the new parish church in 1889. Owing to a falling congregation, St Alban's was made redundant in the 1960s; St Mary's once again became the parish church. St Alban's has found use as a centre for the performing arts.

▲ TEDDINGTON
The Lock c1955
T19007

The motor launch 'Hurlingham' is negotiating the lock at Teddington. A weir is first mentioned here in 1345, and the first lock was built in 1811 with only a single opening for larger craft. The new locks were rebuilt in1904 as double locks, as we see here. The rollers for smaller craft are to the left.

◄ **DETAIL FROM** T19007

TEDDINGTON
Broad Street c1955
T19020

Teddington remained a rural farming area until the arrival of the railway in 1863. New housing and shopping facilities near the station were soon erected. The main shopping centre is in the High Street to the east, leading away from the parish church, and Broad Street to the west. The shops on the left were added onto the front gardens of private houses. Motorists were few in the 1950s, and parking appears to be available for anyone at the kerbside.

▶ **TWICKENHAM**
The Church 1899
43059

The parish church of St Mary's oldest part is the tower, which probably dates from the 14th century. The rest of the church was rebuilt in red brick after the earlier had collapsed in April 1713. The Thames barges are moored alongside Bowyer's wharf, built in 1897 for the storage of coal and corn; they were not finally demolished until 1960, after being criticised for many years for spoiling the river view of the church. The Queen's Head public house on the left can be dated back to the 17th century. It is now called the Barmy Arms.

◀ **TWICKENHAM**
The Ferry 1899 43057

The White Swan public house, first mentioned in 1722, stands on raised ground just beyond the beached punts to the left of centre. Twickenham had two ferry crossings - the Island Ferry over to Eel Pie Island, and Twickenham Ferry itself, plying from the foot of Ferry Road, the slipway on the right, over to Ham on the Surrey shore. This ferry stopped running about 1970. The large building on the right is Mount Lebanon, built in the 1790s. From about 1866 to 1871 this was the residence of Francois, Prince de Joinville, third son of Louis Philippe and father of the Duchesse de Chartres, who lived at Morgan House. Mount Lebanon stood in large grounds alongside Orleans House. The grounds were being sold of for development at beginning of the 20th century; Lebanon House was being used for furniture storage when it burnt down in 1909.

▲ **TWICKENHAM,** *The River 1899* 43058

The photograph was taken from Eel Pie Island, facing towards the parish church and C Shore's boathouse and Island Ferry. C Hammertons, who continued operating the ferry and hiring out canoes, punts and dinghies, took over Shore's in 1926.

◄ **TWICKENHAM**
The River c1955
T91036

The island ferry was largely superseded by the construction of Snappers footbridge in 1957. The main channel of the Thames is on the Surrey side of Eel Pie Island.

TWICKENHAM
London Road c1955
T91022

The railway station at Twickenham was opened in 1848, and the shopping district quickly developed nearby; it was gradually being improved with new shops in the late Victorian and early Edwardian period. York Street, on the right to the other side of the Midland Bank, was cut through only at the end of the 19th century to improve traffic flow to Richmond; traffic previously had to funnel through the narrow Church Street, to the right of Barclays Bank.

▼ **THAMES DITTON**, *The Swan Hotel, Summer Road c1955* T103018

The Swan is well known to boating people, and especially anglers. Among its many frequenters none was fonder of this riverside resort than Thomas Hook, who penned 'The Song of the Shirt'. The Swan's lawn commands a pretty view of the river and of the grounds of Hampton Court Palace. The Swan is Grade I listed. There is a public slipway to the right. Beyond the pub are the Ferry Works, originally built in 1879 by the engineering firm of Willand & Robinson. Owing to a large fire in 1888, the works were rebuilt using the then innovative 'saw tooth' roof design to allow light onto the shop floor. After Willand & Robinson moved to Rugby in 1911, Auto Carriers (makers of the AC cars of later fame) occupied the buildings. After the Second World War, invalid cars made of fibreglass were manufactured here for the Ministry of Pensions. A variety of firms now operate from here.

► **THAMES DITTON**
High Street c1955 T103011

The small post office (right) catering for local needs moved to No 42, High Street in 1936. Next door, Leonard North's garage was serving National Benzole petrol; at this time an attendant would fill up for you - self service at petrol stations was still about 15 years into the future. The National Benzole Company was formed in 1919 to market motor benzole, a by-product of coal carbonisation; by 1950 there were over 250 plants associated with the steel industry and gas works. For motor cars it was blended with petrol and retailed as National Benzole. The two white rings on the tree (right) were painted at the beginning of the Second World War as an aid to motorists during the blackout, and by the time of this photograph had only just begun to fade.

◄ **THAMES DITTON**
High Street c1967
T103054

With the decline of coking coal as a fuel, benzole production fell, and in 1957 National Benzole was acquired by Shell-Mex & BP Ltd - and Leonard North's garage is now selling Shell petrol. The large tree in the middle of the roadway had been felled in December 1955 and replaced with a young sapling. Mr Clifford Oxley Hill took over the post office on 13 May 1967.

► **THAMES DITTON**
The Bridge c1960 T103045

This is the private footbridge to the island at Thames Ditton. The notice states that both the bridge and the island are private. The island, once deserted, is now almost totally covered by small chalets and bungalows, with boats moored on the riverside.

THAMES DITTON
St Nicholas' Church c1955 T103014

The church is first mentioned around 1120 as belonging to Merton Priory. The bell tower and part of the chancel wall are from this period. At least six stages of extensions and rebuilding, including a major though sympathetic re-building in the mid Victorian period, result in the church we see today. Of special interest are the font (early Norman) and the Doom painting above the chancel arch. Three bells are mentioned in an inventory in 1552; the ring was increased to six in 1753-54 by Thomas Swaine of Longford. The church is famous for its brasses: five groups depict about 70 figures dating from the 16th century – one brass, of William Notte and his wife, shows 19 children. The bells were re-cast in 1962 by Taylor's and re-hung in a new hardwood frame in 1980.

RICHMOND PARK
c1955 R31035

The royal connections with this park probably go back further than with other parks, beginning with Edward I (1272-1307), when the area was part of the Manor of Shene; the name was changed to Richmond during Henry VII's reign. In 1625 Charles I brought his court to Richmond Palace to escape the plague in London, and turned the park into a private hunting ground for red and fallow deer. His decision to enclose the land with a high wall in 1637 was not popular

with the local residents and landowners. It occupies 2,500 acres in parts of Richmond, Kingston, Mortlake and Putney parishes, the largest open space in London. There are about 600 deer in the park today, 350 fallow and 250 red deer; but in the 1660s there were 2,000. From Richmond Park's highest point, St Paul's cathedral can be seen 12 miles away. Essential to its character is the rich landscape of semi-natural acidic grassland, with areas of bog and bracken, wetland, woodland and ancient parkland trees. In 1992 the park was designated as a Site of Special Scientific Interest by English Nature.

INDEX

NAMES OF SUBSCRIBERS

R Abbey and Family

The Adcroft Family

Margaret B Austen

Sheila & Geoff Austin of Kingston

J & P Brett

In memory of W Burden

Mr & Mrs J P Burton

Claire & David, Kingston

P Cooney

John Douglas

A tribute to my parents - Dot & Sid Eastop

A E Farthing

Mr & Mrs T D French

Michael Gray

The Griffiths Family, Chessington

The Gudge Family, Kingston

Alan Hamilton

Andy & Michelle Hinds, New Malden

Mr F Howe

The Johnston Family

Martin P Jones

Kingston Museum & Heritage Service

Kingston Guardian

Mr & Mrs J Kittle, Kingston

Joan P Little

Jeff P Littlemore

B Lucus

Mr & Mrs Merton

Jane Murray

Joan Norton

Stuart P Read

The Robinson Family

D J & J Rolfe

P J Sampson

The Schwier Family, Twickenham, love Julia

P Shepherd

Ian P Smith

Enid & Peter Smits

Mr & Mrs Taylor

The Wakeling Family

Mark & Sue Walsh

W R Weaver

Lucy, Peter & Jane Welch

The Western Family

The Wiggins Family

The Wilson Family

Gary & Kirstie Wilson, Kingston 1998-04

FRITH PRODUCTS & SERVICES

Francis Frith would doubtless be pleased to know that the pioneering publishing venture he started in 1860 still continues today. Over a hundred and forty years later, The Francis Frith Collection continues in the same innovative tradition and is now one of the foremost publishers of vintage photographs in the world. Some of the current activities include:

Interior Decoration

Today Frith's photographs can be seen framed and as giant wall murals in thousands of pubs, restaurants, hotels, banks, retail stores and other public buildings throughout the country. In every case they enhance the unique local atmosphere of the places they depict and provide reminders of gentler days in an increasingly busy and frenetic world.

Product Promotions

Frith products are used by many major companies to promote the sales of their own products or to reinforce their own history and heritage. Frith promotions have been used by Hovis bread, Courage beers, Scots Porage Oats, Colman's mustard, Cadbury's foods, Mellow Birds coffee, Dunhill pipe tobacco, Guinness, and Bulmer's Cider.

Genealogy and Family History

As the interest in family history and roots grows world-wide, more and more people are turning to Frith's photographs of Great Britain for images of the towns, villages and streets where their ancestors lived; and, of course, photographs of the churches and chapels where their ancestors were christened, married and buried are an essential part of every genealogy tree and family album.

Frith Products

All Frith photographs are available Framed or just as Mounted Prints and Posters (size 23 x 16 inches). These may be ordered from the address below. From time to time other products - Address Books, Calendars, Table Mats, etc - are available.

The Internet

Already fifty thousand Frith photographs can be viewed and purchased on the internet through the Frith websites and a myriad of partner sites.

For more detailed information on Frith companies and products, look at these sites:

www.francisfrith.co.uk
www.francisfrith.com
(for North American visitors)

See the complete list of Frith Books at:
www.francisfrith.co.uk

This web site is regularly updated with the latest list of publications from the Frith Book Company. If you wish to buy books relating to another part of the country that your local bookshop does not stock, you may purchase on-line.

For further information, trade, or author enquiries please contact us at the address below:
The Francis Frith Collection, Frith's Barn, Teffont, Salisbury, Wiltshire, England SP3 5QP.
Tel: +44 (0)1722 716 376 Fax: +44 (0)1722 716 881 Email: sales@francisfrith.co.uk

See Frith books on the internet at www.francisfrith.co.uk

FREE PRINT OF YOUR CHOICE

Mounted Print
Overall size 14 x 11 inches (355 x 280mm)

Choose any Frith photograph in this book.
Simply complete the Voucher opposite and return it with your remittance for £2.25 (to cover postage and handling) and we will print the photograph of your choice in SEPIA (size 11 x 8 inches) and supply it in a cream mount with a burgundy rule line (overall size 14 x 11 inches).
Please note: photographs with a reference number starting with a "Z" are not Frith photographs and cannot be supplied under this offer.
Offer valid for delivery to UK addresses only.

PLUS: **Order additional Mounted Prints at HALF PRICE - £7.49 each** (normally £14.99)
If you would like to order more Frith prints from this book, possibly as gifts for friends and family, you can buy them at half price (with no additional postage and handling costs).

PLUS: **Have your Mounted Prints framed**
For an extra £14.95 per print you can have your mounted print(s) framed in an elegant polished wood and gilt moulding, overall size 16 x 13 inches (no additional postage and handling required).

IMPORTANT!

These special prices are only available if you use this form to order . You must use the ORIGINAL VOUCHER on this page (no copies permitted). We can only despatch to one address. This offer cannot be combined with any other offer.

Send completed Voucher form to:
The Francis Frith Collection, Frith's Barn, Teffont, Salisbury, Wiltshire SP3 5QP

CHOOSE A PHOTOGRAPH FROM THIS BOOK

Voucher for **FREE** and Reduced Price Frith Prints

Please do not photocopy this voucher. Only the original is valid, so please fill it in, cut it out and return it to us with your order.

Picture ref no	Page no	Qty	Mounted @ £7.49	Framed + £14.95	Total Cost
		1	Free of charge*	£	£
			£7.49	£	£
			£7.49	£	£
			£7.49	£	£
			£7.49	£	£
			£7.49	£	£
Please allow 28 days for delivery			* Post & handling (UK)		£2.25
			Total Order Cost		£

Title of this book . . . .

I enclose a cheque/postal order for £ . . . .
made payable to 'The Francis Frith Collection'

OR please debit my Mastercard / Visa / Switch (Maestro) /Amex card
(credit cards please on all overseas orders), details below

Card Number

Issue No (Switch only)   Valid from (Amex/Switch)

Expires   Signature

Name Mr/Mrs/Ms . . . .
Address . . . .
. . . .
. . . .
. . . . Postcode . . . .
Daytime Tel No . . . .
Email . . . .

Valid to 31/12/07

Free Print – see overleaf

Would you like to find out more about Francis Frith?

We have recently recruited some entertaining speakers who are happy to visit local groups, clubs and societies to give an illustrated talk documenting Frith's travels and photographs. If you are a member of such a group and are interested in hosting a presentation, we would love to hear from you.

Our speakers bring with them a small selection of our local town and county books, together with sample prints. They are happy to take orders. A small proportion of the order value is donated to the group who have hosted the presentation. The talks are therefore an excellent way of fundraising for small groups and societies.

Can you help us with information about any of the Frith photographs in this book?

We are gradually compiling an historical record for each of the photographs in the Frith archive. It is always fascinating to find out the names of the people shown in the pictures, as well as insights into the shops, buildings and other features depicted.

If you recognize anyone in the photographs in this book, or if you have information not already included in the author's caption, do let us know. We would love to hear from you, and will try to publish it in future books or articles.

Our production team

Frith books are produced by a small dedicated team at offices in the converted Grade II listed 18th-century barn at Teffont near Salisbury, illustrated above. Most have worked with the Frith Collection for many years. All have in common one quality: they have a passion for the Frith Collection. The team is constantly expanding, but currently includes:

Paul Baron, Phillip Brennan, Jason Buck, John Buck, Ruth Butler, Heather Crisp, David Davies, Louis du Mont, Isobel Hall, Gareth Harris, Lucy Hart, Julian Hight, Peter Horne, James Kinnear, Karen Kinnear, Tina Leary, Stuart Login, David Marsh, Lesley-Ann Millard, Sue Molloy, Glenda Morgan, Wayne Morgan, Sarah Roberts, Kate Rotondetto, Dean Scource, Eliza Sackett, Terence Sackett, Sandra Sampson, Adrian Sanders, Sandra Sanger, Jan Scrivens, Julia Skinner, David Smith, Miles Smith, Lewis Taylor, Shelley Tolcher, Lorraine Tuck, Amanita Wainwright and Ricky Williams.